Kickstands UP

Carol J. Cooper

Artist's credit: Carol J. Cooper, Bob Campbell, Sharon A. Jewell, Kim Briggs

Archway Publishing books may be ordered through booksellers or by contacting:

Archway Publishing
1663 Liberty Drive
Bloomington, IN 47403
www.archwaypublishing.com
1 (888) 242-5904

ISBN: 978-1-4808-7327-8 (sc)
ISBN: 978-1-4808-7326-1 (e)

Print information available on the last page.

Archway Publishing rev. date: 02/18/2019

Dedication

I would like to dedicate this book with love to my grandson, Orion, who through the eyes of a wondering child, is always fascinated with Gramma's motorcycle!

Acknowledgments

With much gratitude, I would like to thank Kim Urbanosky-Briggs, Bob Campbell, and Sharon Jewell for the generous use of their photographs in this project.

Thank you, Kenna Kenworthy, for your support and the first critical edits of the initial manuscripts. Your encouragement and excitement carried me through!

A HUGE "thank you" to my beautiful daughter-in-law, Cassandra Cooper, for your never ending patience, determination, and amazing talents in getting all of the photos correctly sized and ready to go. Love you!

Finally, a heartfelt thank you to every brother and sister biker that I have had the priviledge of learning from, riding with, and holding in my heart. YOU truly are the inspiration for this book.

People sometimes do not understand motorcycle riders– or bikers, as they are called, but I am here to tell you that we are like everybody else! We have mothers, fathers, sons, and daughters; people whom we love and hold in our hearts, just as you do.

The Singletary Family

Another thing that people don't realize is that we have careers and jobs, just like your parents. I have ridden with nurses, scientists, salesmen, chefs, carpenters; and people are always very surprised to hear that I am a kindergarten teacher!

My kindergarten classroom

There is something about riding a motorcycle that comes from deep down within the heart and soul. It gives the rider much joy, a sense of freedom, and release from any problems or stress. You may get this same feeling when riding your skateboard, playing soccer, or just from being with your friends.

Just like you study different kinds of weather at school, bikers do also every time they ride. They check the weather forecast before they take a trip to see what the weather conditions will be. It may be too hot, or too cold, and no biker likes to ride in the rain. The raindrops actually feel like little pins on your skin from the force of the wind!

I have even ridden in the slippery snow while traveling high up in the mountains of California. Riders have to be very careful when traveling on wet or slick roads and bridges.

Grand Teton mountain range

bridge over Bull Shoals Lake

In school, students are taught to be kind and respectful to others and treat them the way they would like to be treated. It is the same with bikers. We meet many, many new people every time we ride. Sometimes we ride alone, and other times we enjoy the company of friends. But, no matter where we go, we treat everyone nicely and help others whenever needed.

bike rally

Helping may be through volunteering, participating in benefits, or donations. Bikers are also very active in their support for the United States, veterans, and soldiers who have fought so valiantly for our rights as citizens. You may often see bikers at parades, military funerals, and as escorts for our brave servicemen and women.

Veteran's Day parade

Students spend a lot of time learning about their 5 senses in school. (see, smell, taste, hear, and touch) Bikers use each and every one of them every time they ride, with the most important sense being sight. They must stay very alert, scanning everything around with their eyes, ready to respond and react in an instant if necessary.

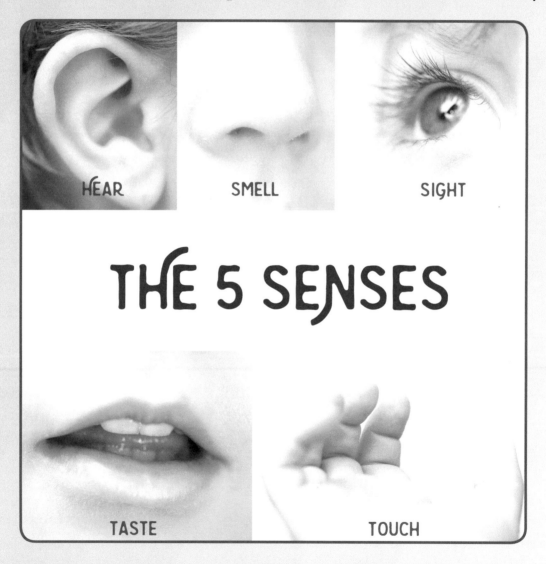

HEAR

SMELL

SIGHT

THE 5 SENSES

TASTE

TOUCH

Sometimes their hearts are moved by the breathtaking beauty that they see while riding winding roads, along coastal beaches, or through canyons and forests. Bikers are always amazed at the wonders of nature, whether it be the delicate spring flowers, the brilliant colors of the fall leaves, or the incredible animals and creatures that we share this world with.

colorful flowers

Oak Trees in the Fall

I love to feel the warm sun on my face, and the cool winds blowing through my hair as I ride. I can also feel the vibration of the bike through the handlebars, and through the seat.

riding up the California coast

As bikers go along their journeys and pass homes, they can often smell bacon cooking in kitchens, sweet flowers growing beside the road, or smell the freshly cut grass and hay. I think my favorite fragrance is that of wood burning in fireplaces on a cool, crisp autumn day.

hay bales

People tease us, and say that we "ride to eat- and eat to ride" because it always seems like bikers end up going to a restaurant to dine with friends. Just like you enjoy going to your favorite places to eat with your family, bikers enjoy good food and the fellowship of close friends.

Bikers listen to the sound of their bike's engine because it tells them when to shift up or down. They also listen carefully to the sounds of the traffic around them, always alert.

Harley engine

Another very important thing bikers must know are the traffic signs and laws. You have studied them in social studies. Bikers must remember and apply them every time they ride their motorcycles. They have the same laws as the cars, and the police will pull them over and give them a ticket if they do not obey them.

55 mph speed limit

winding road

Safety is extremely important, and it begins with always wearing a helmet to protect their heads, just like you do when you ride your bicycle. They also check their bikes before they ride to make sure the lights and brakes all work and there is the correct amount of air pressure in the tires. We call that "a safety check."

One year, my friends and I planned a very fun and exciting trip across the country on our motorcycles, just like you may plan a vacation with your family. We traveled from California to a little town in South Dakota, named Sturgis. We were amazed at the thousands and thousands of motorcycles there!

town of Sturgis

Our group rode all across The Badlands and stopped to see majestic landmarks like Mount Rushmore, the Crazy Horse Monument, and Yellowstone National Park.

Mount Rushmore National Memorial

Crazy Horse

Yellowstone National Park

The park ranger warned us to turn off our motorcycles if any herds of buffalo were crossing the roads around us. We took his advice, and were awestruck as the huge herds of these massive beasts passed so closely to us!

Buffalo at Yellowstone National Park

We also saw beautiful waterfalls, bubbling hot springs, and gushing geysers, including its most famous, Old Faithful. Our incredible journey covered 4,000 miles, and ended with crossing the hot Mojave Desert.

Old Faithful

I hope I have helped you understand the joys of riding a motorcycle and that you can see that bikers are just like everyone else. The next time you see one of us riding, please feel free to wave or say "hi!" We even have a special wave that we use when passing another biker while riding. We feel like our fellow riders are "our brothers and sisters" of the road, kind of like one huge family. When you wave to us, you become a part of that wonderful family, too! Kickstands up- let's **go**!

me sitting on bike

Afterword

Come With Me

For those of you who do not ride and have not received "this calling" that many of us share, let me paint you a picture and take you "with me" on a ride. I don't know what is better, the freshness of the cool air, or... the hum of the bike's powerful engine. Every sense becomes enhanced and enlightened and all of life's trappings vanish from your thoughts. You become "one with the bike" as you lean into the corners together, anticipating the approaching curves in the roads. At times it almost feels like you are on the wings of the soaring hawks above, gliding along effortlessly as they grace the blue sky.

The rolling hillsides spread before your eyes, going on for miles in a beautiful tapestry of green hues. I cross several bridges that recently tried their best to contain and hold back the raging waters from the recent torrential rains. Now, these creeks and streams are once more calm, calling you gently to them. The trees share the comfort of their shade, at times almost making a canopy overhead. Their shadows and light form patterns on the pavement, which at times almost appear puzzle-like. I smile as I carefully avoid a Box Turtle, admiring its steadfast determination to make it to its destination.

One road led to the local fish hatchery, and I could see many black silhouetted shadows, each representing a trout silently swimming in motion against the rapid current. The water felt ice cold as I leaned in to splash it onto my tingling skin. I stood in awe and watched a waterfall cascading with strength and force over the rocky wall. The sunlight seemed "to dance" on the ripples of water that flowed between the tree lined shore. It was only the pending end of the day that called me to leave this place of peace and serenity.

The sun was an incredible huge ball of orange and magenta hues, hanging low in the sky before me. The sky was draped in majestic colors of soft pastels. How can you not feel the touch from the mighty hand of God as you marvel at these awesome displays? Some days I ride with my group, but on this day I rode as a "lone wolf" and was blessed with the gifts that it brought.

Printed in the United States
By Bookmasters